No part of this book may be reproduced,
Stored in a retrieval system. Or transmitted by
Any means without the written permission of
The author. Martha E Benzler
Published By Createspace.com
IBSN: 13-978- 1515232322
IBSN: 10-1515232328
L, of C Control Number: VA-1-340-702
Printed in the United States of America

This book is for my friends

Sea Mack Bassirian &

Tom from the R. M. Library

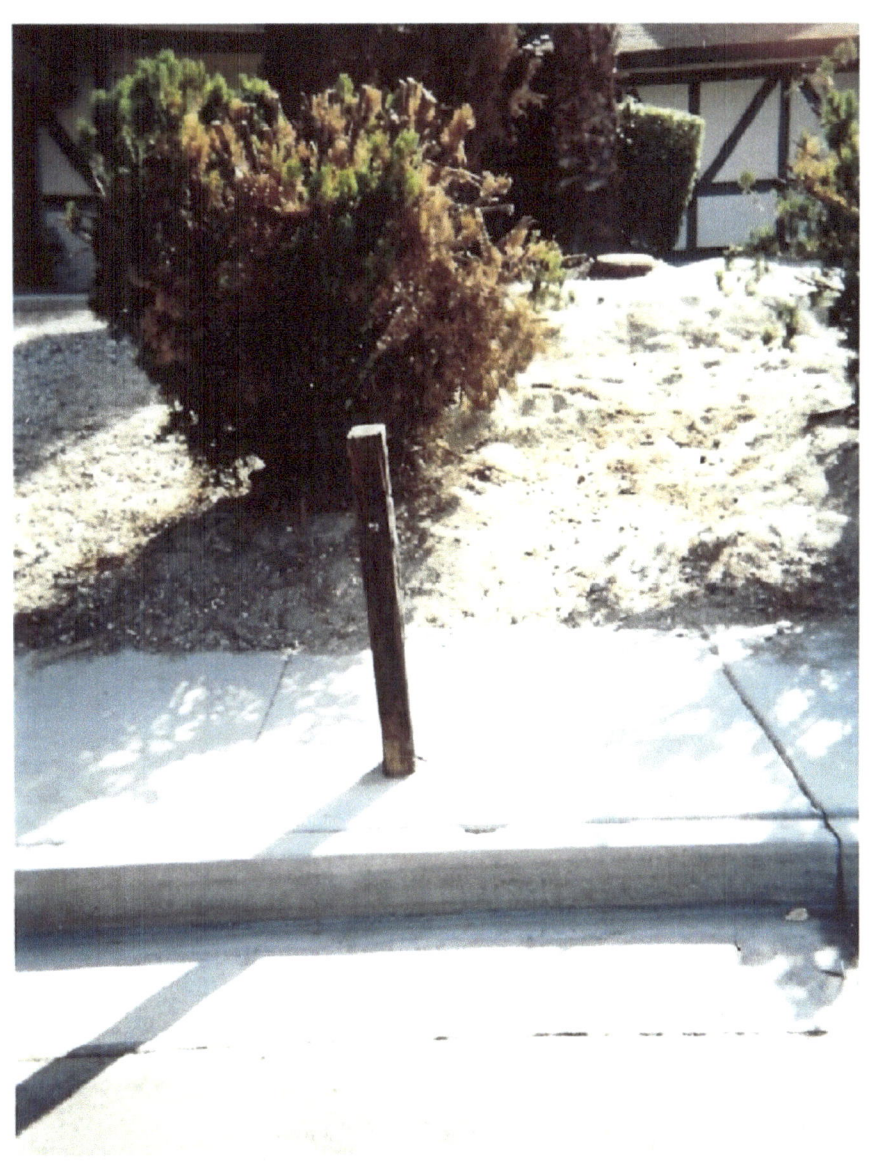

**This is the mail box post
That gave me the ideal for this Book
(1)**

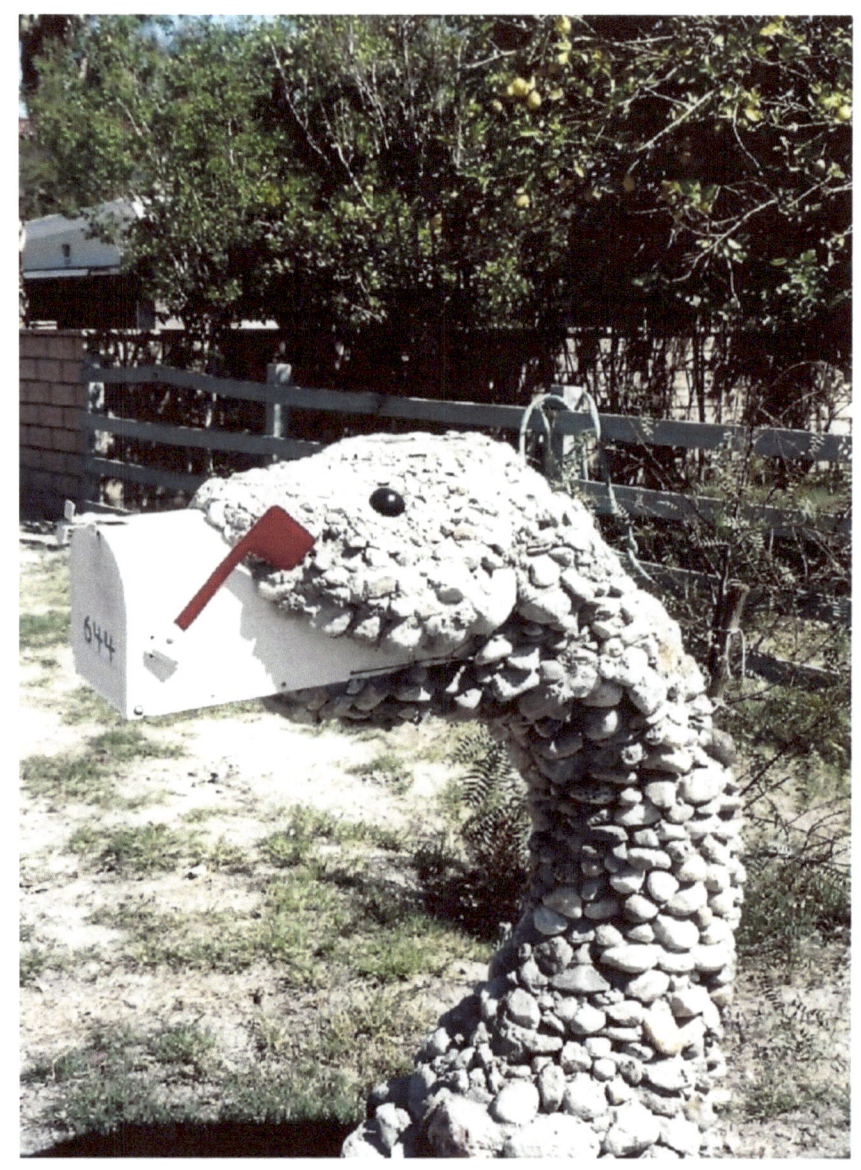

(2)

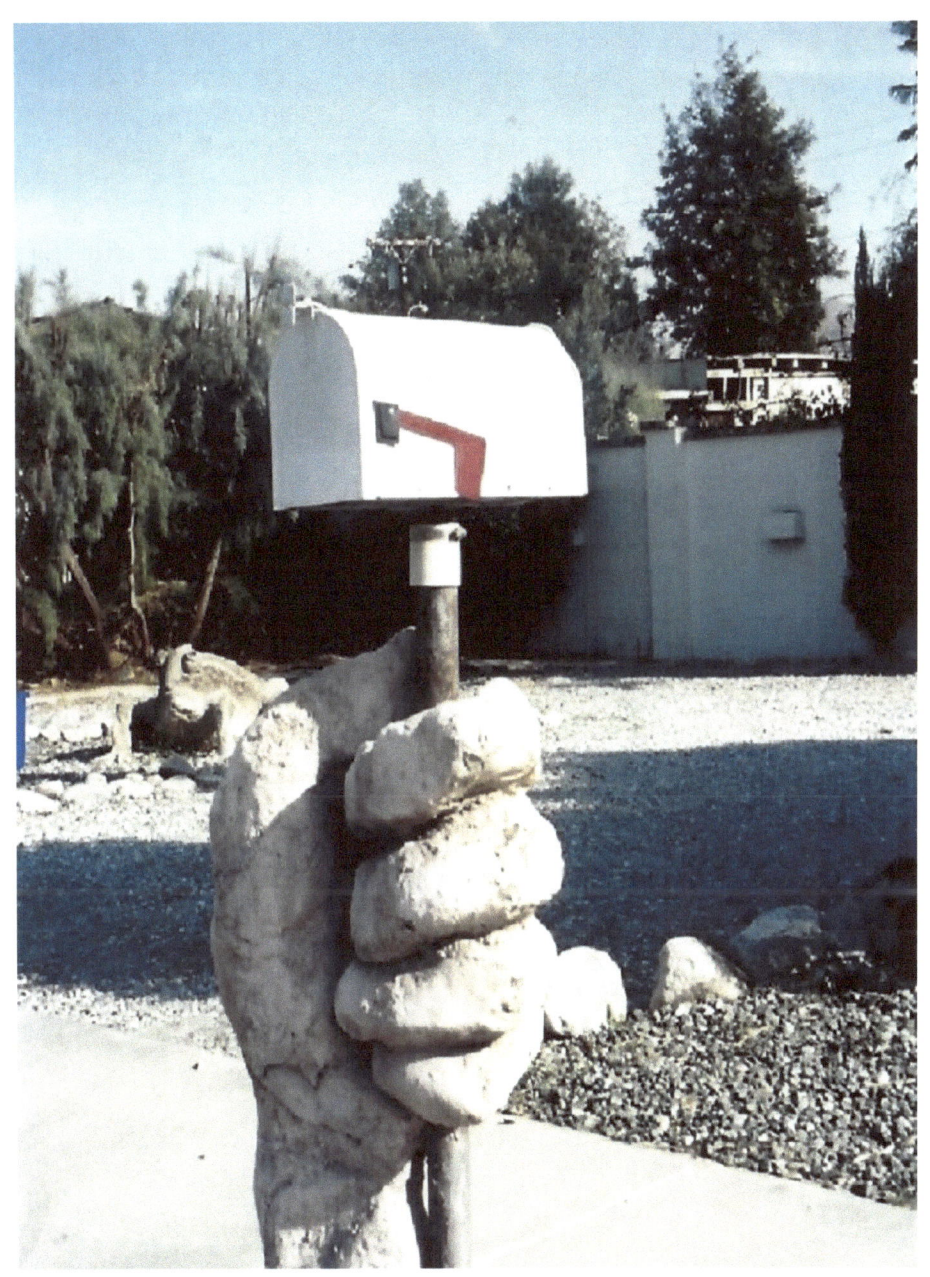

(3)

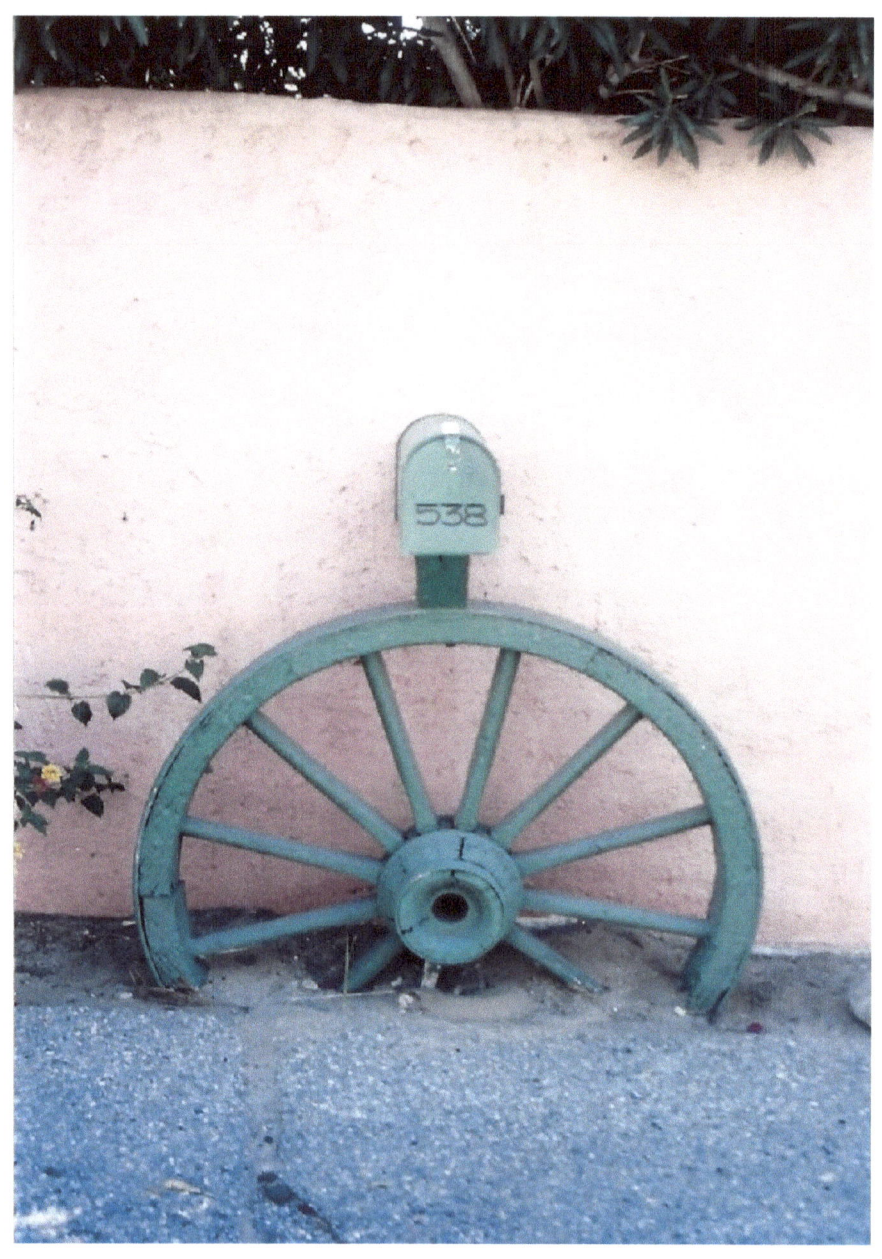

(4)

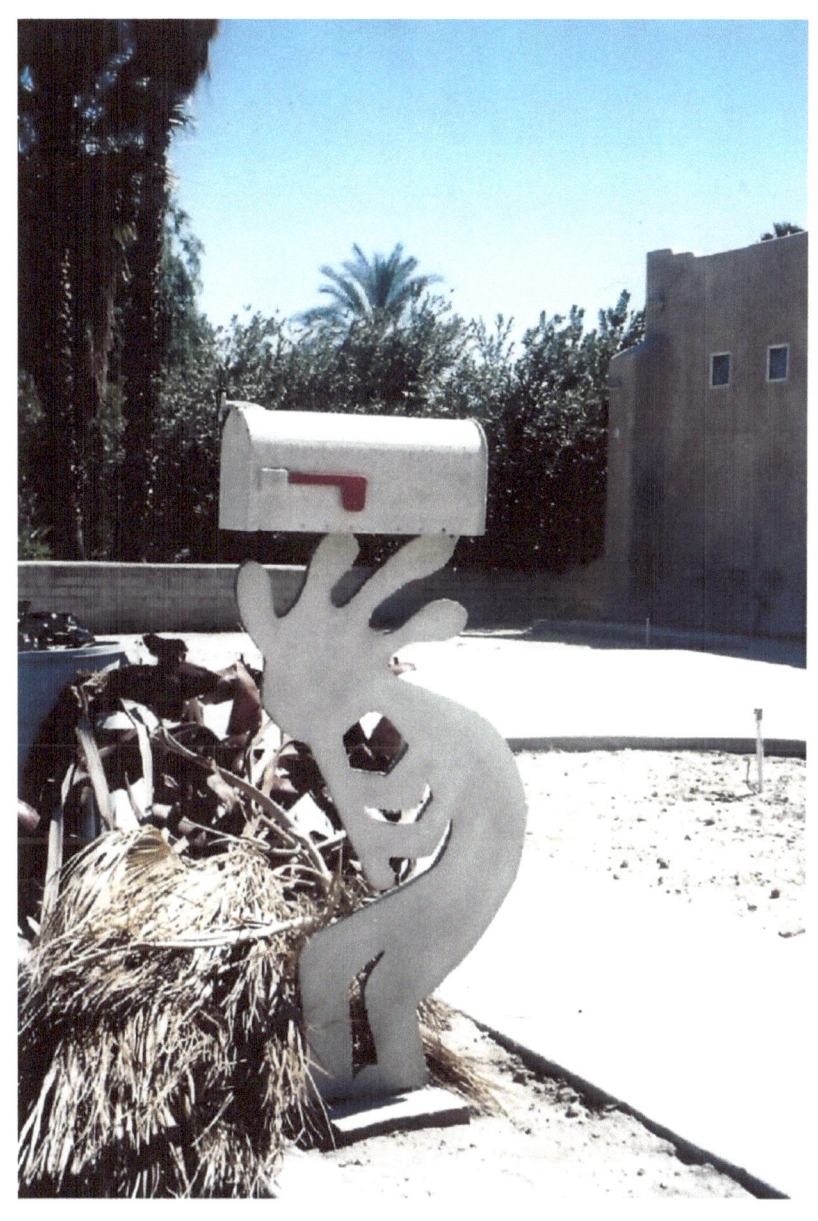

(5)

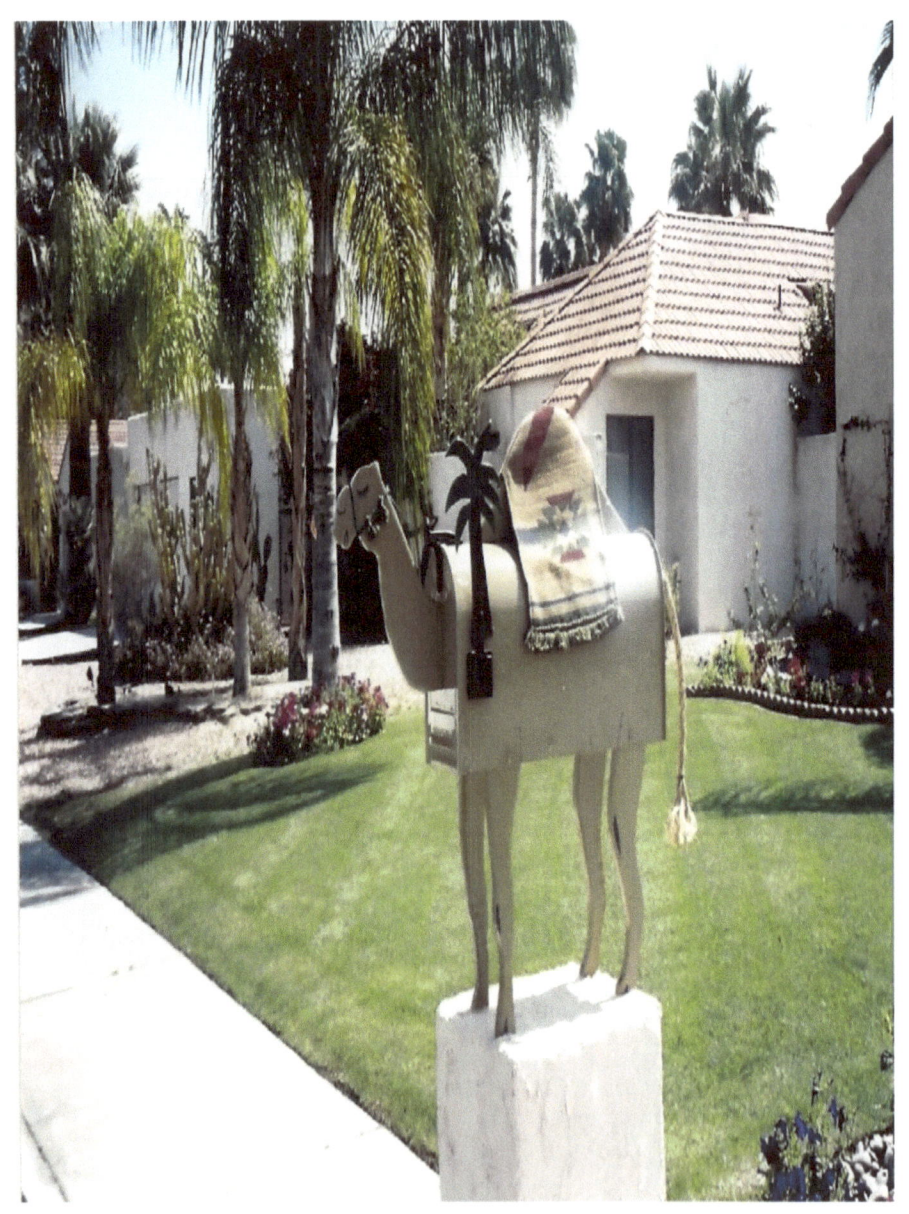

(6)

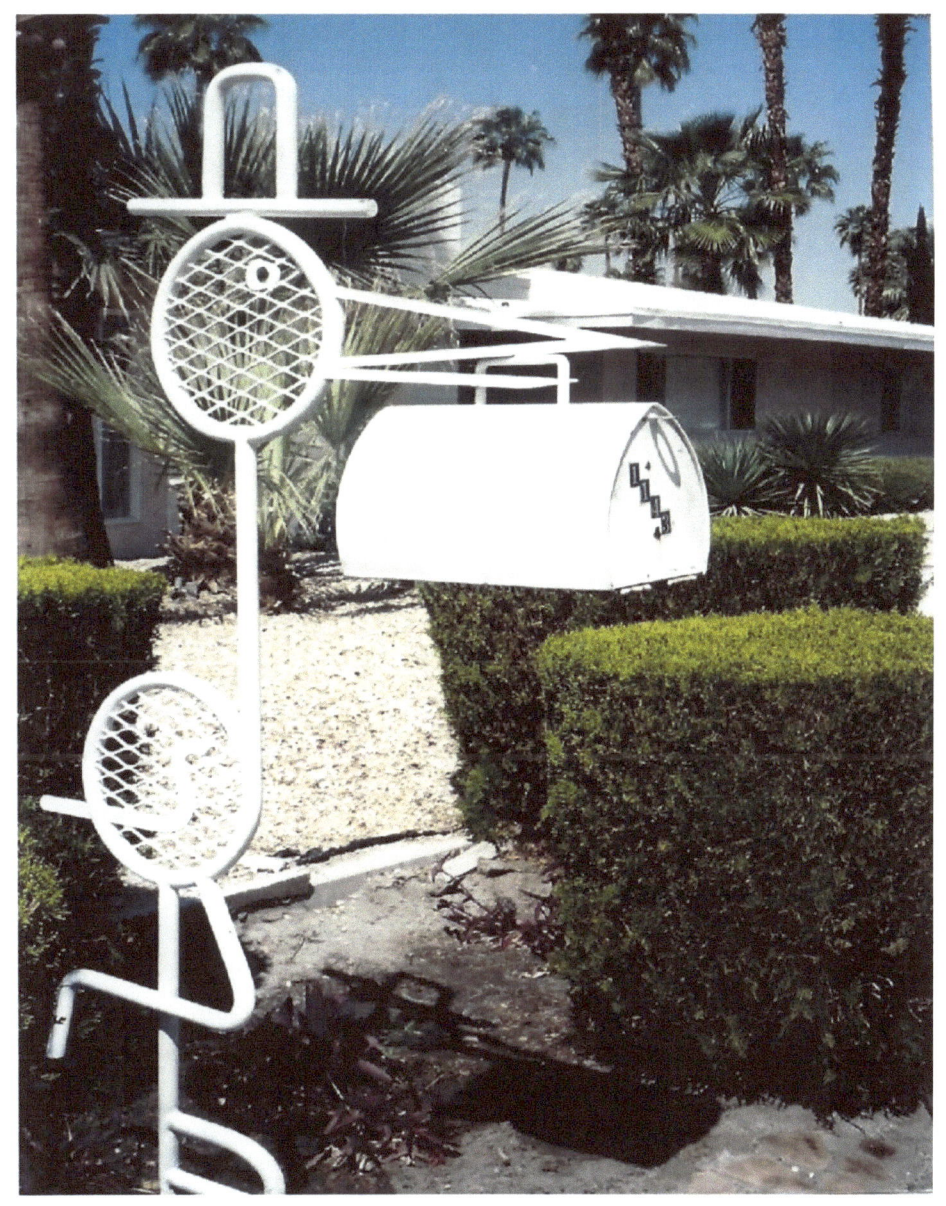

(7)

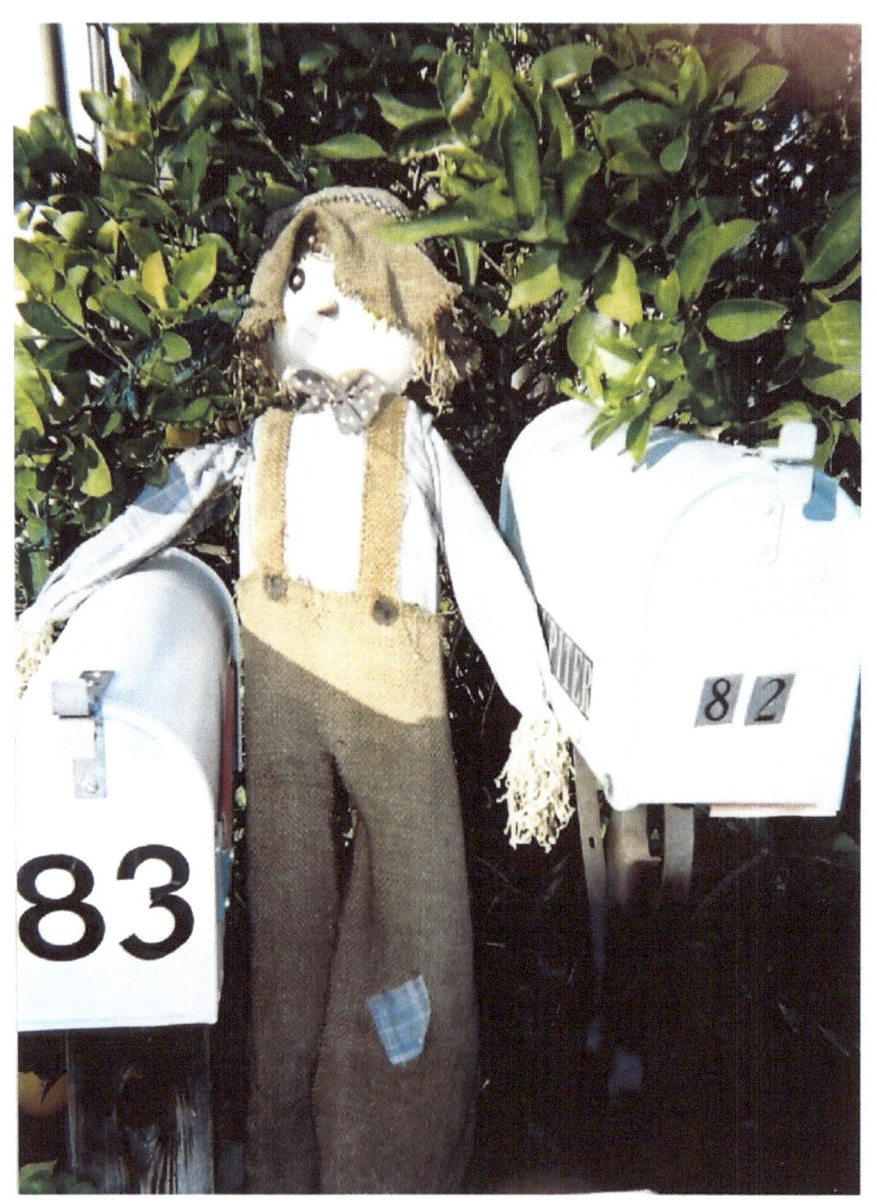

(8)

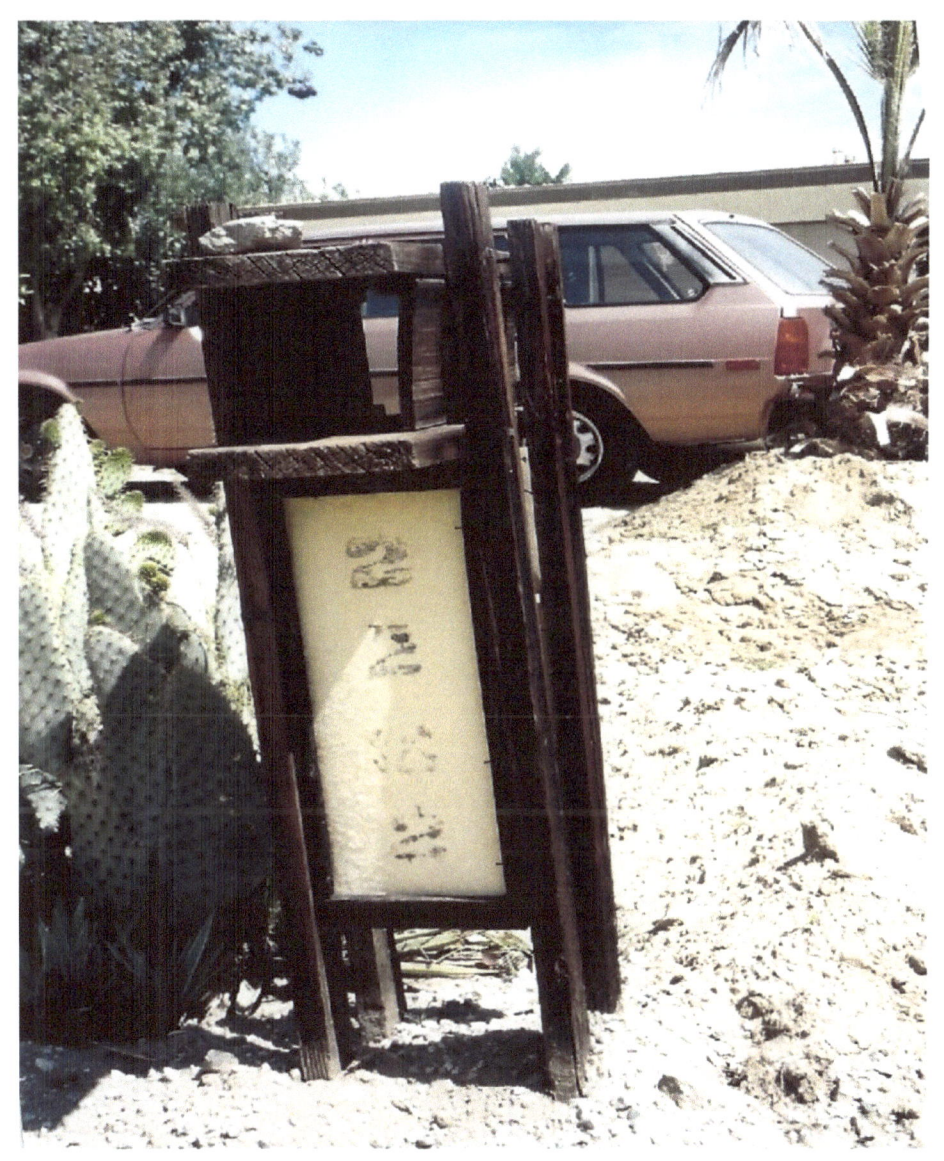

(9)

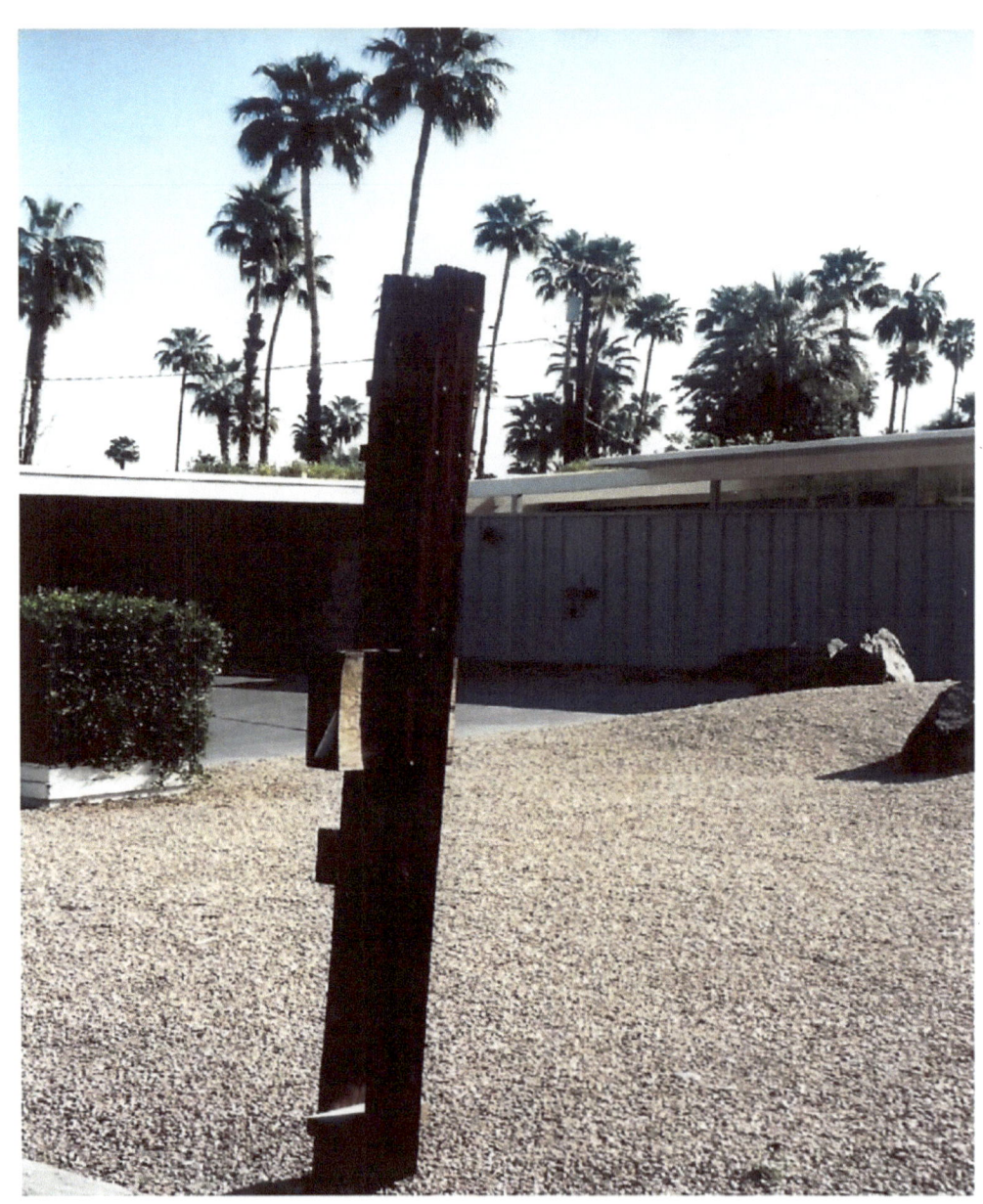

(10)

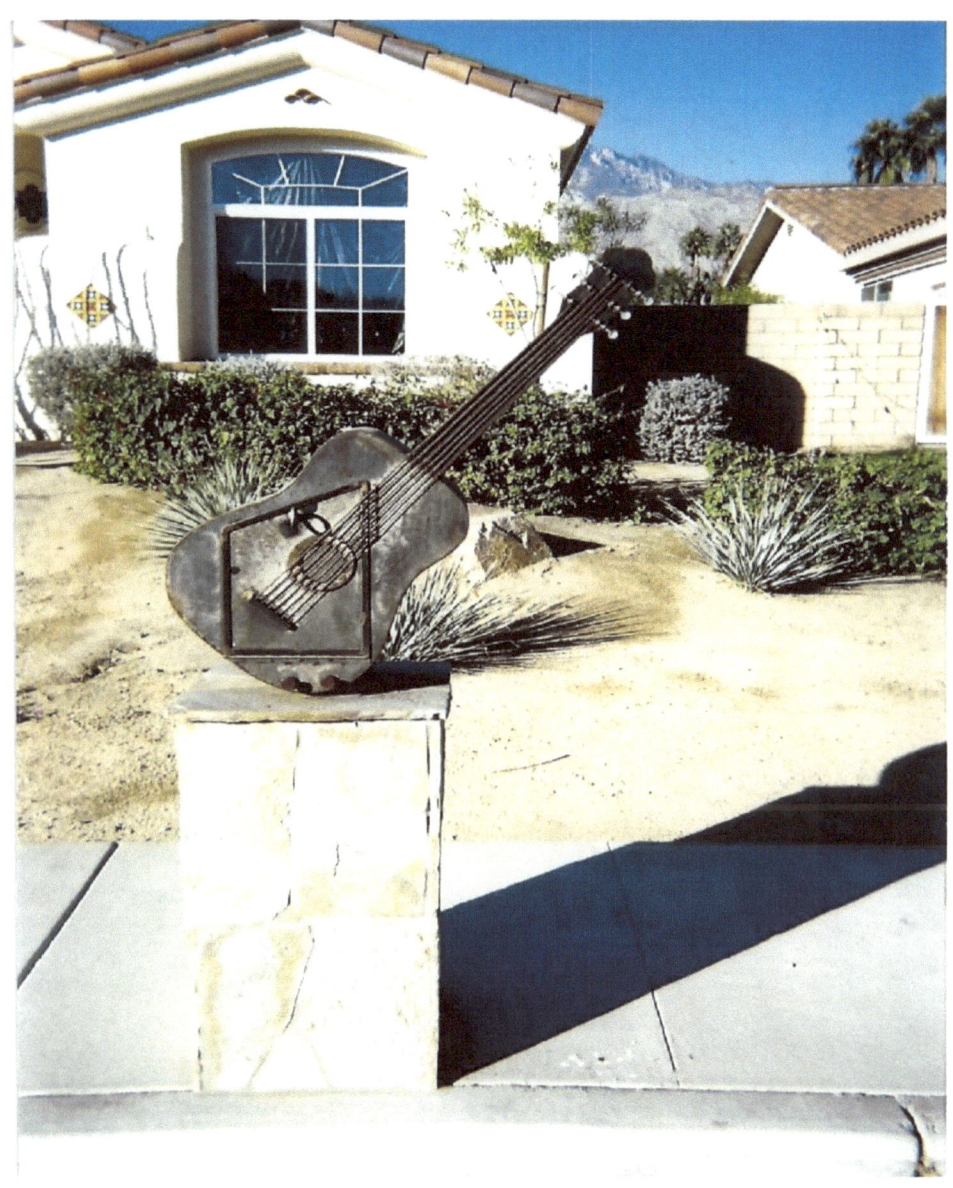

(11)

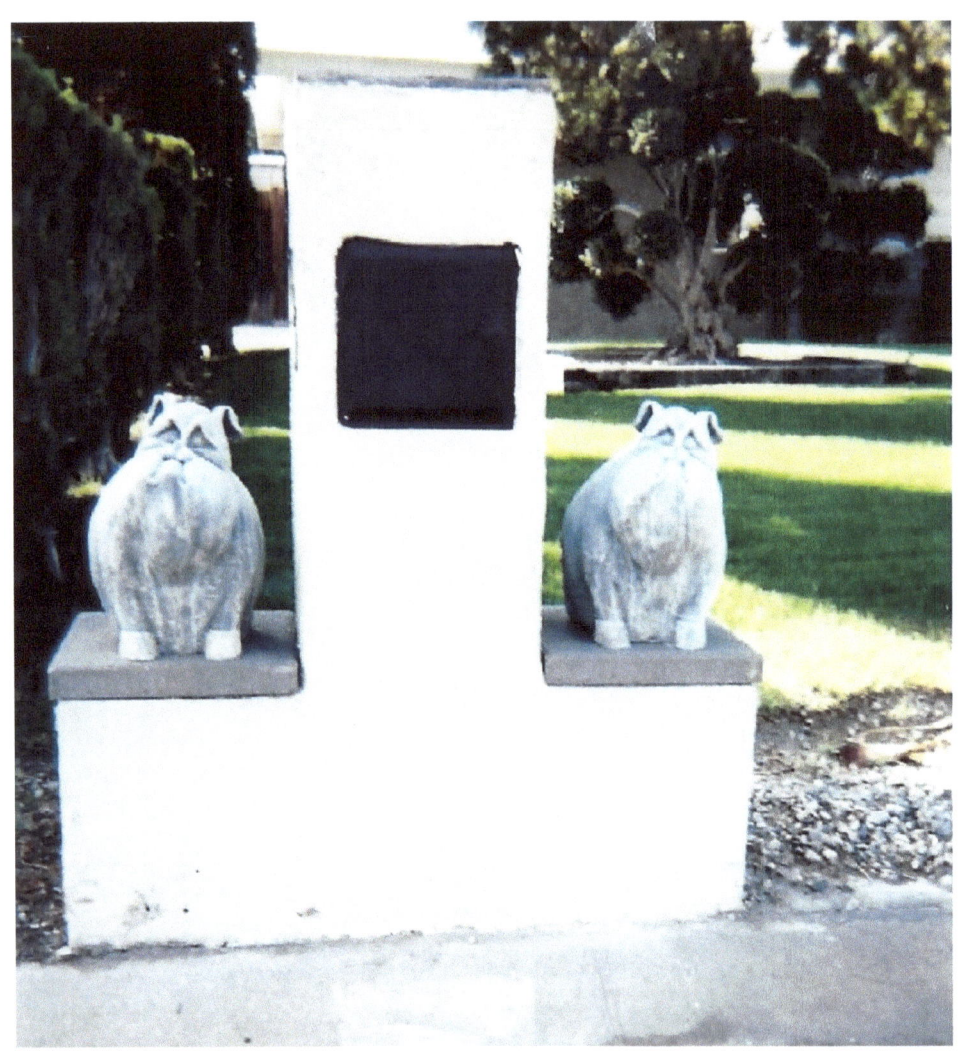

(12)

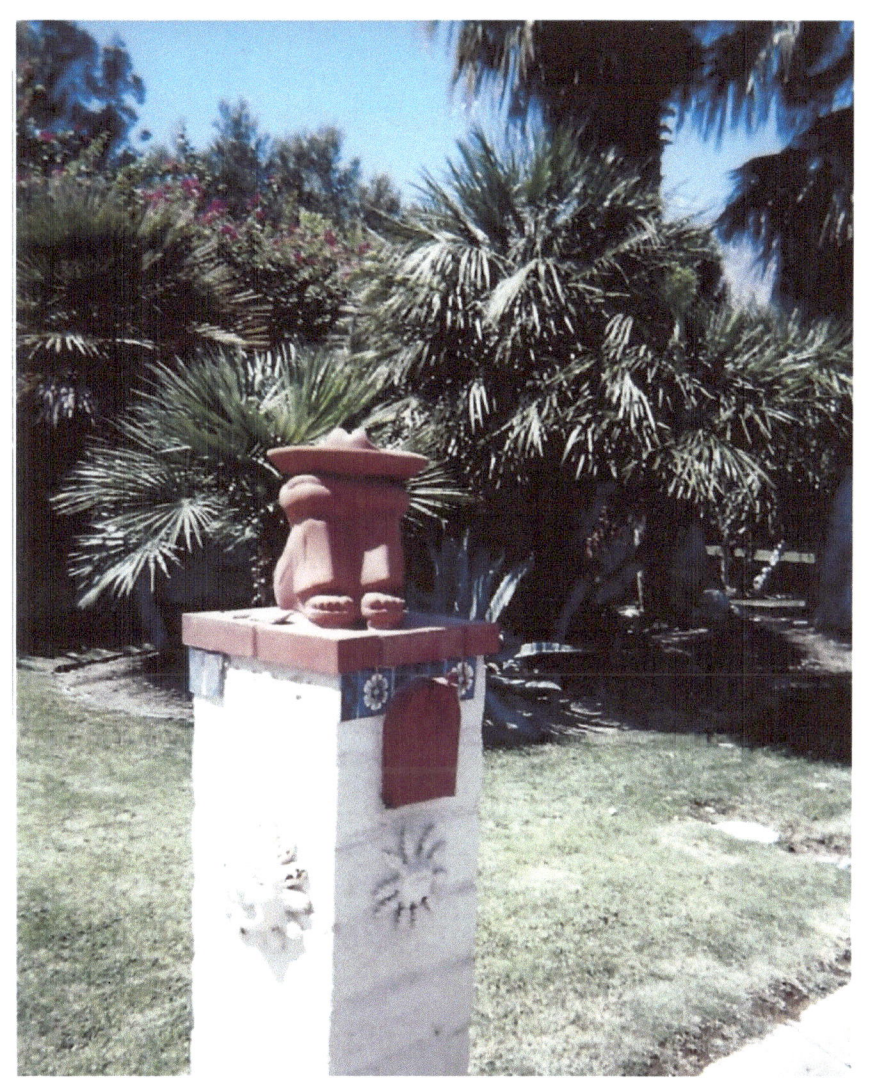

(13)

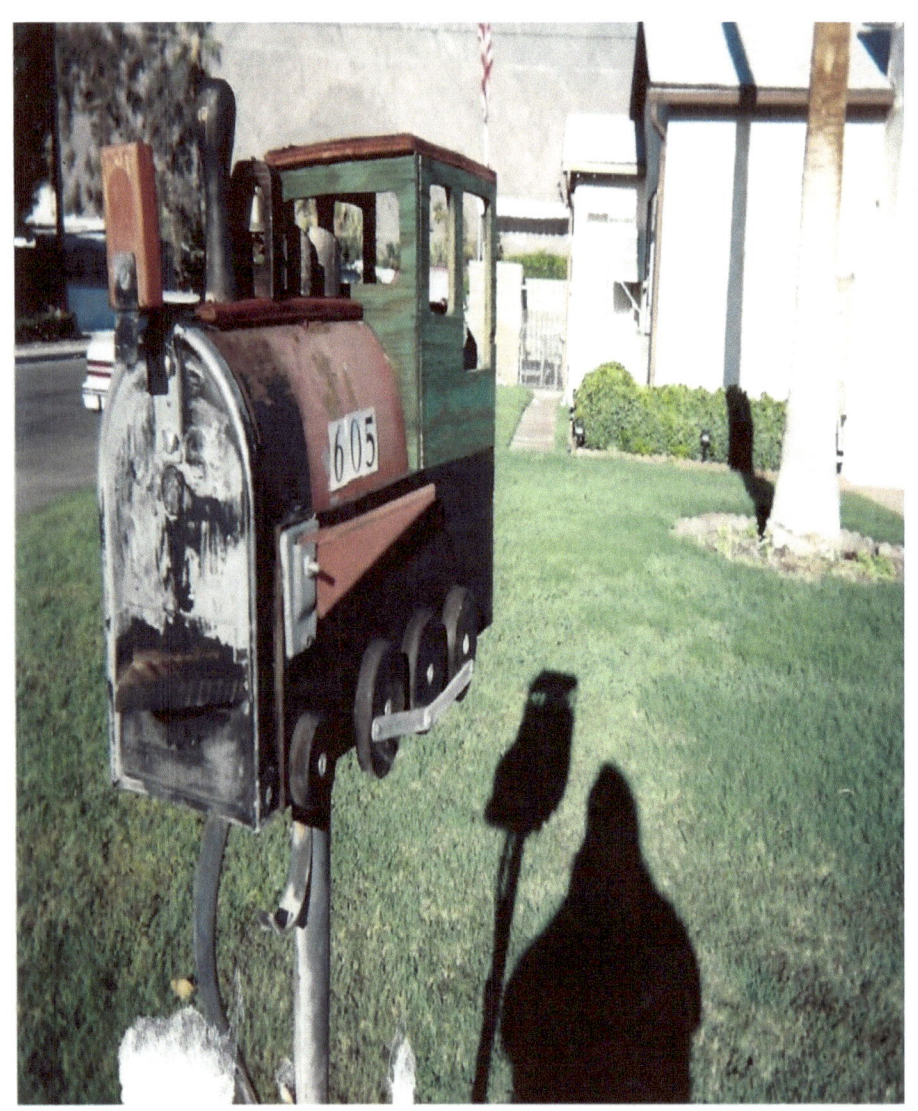

(14)

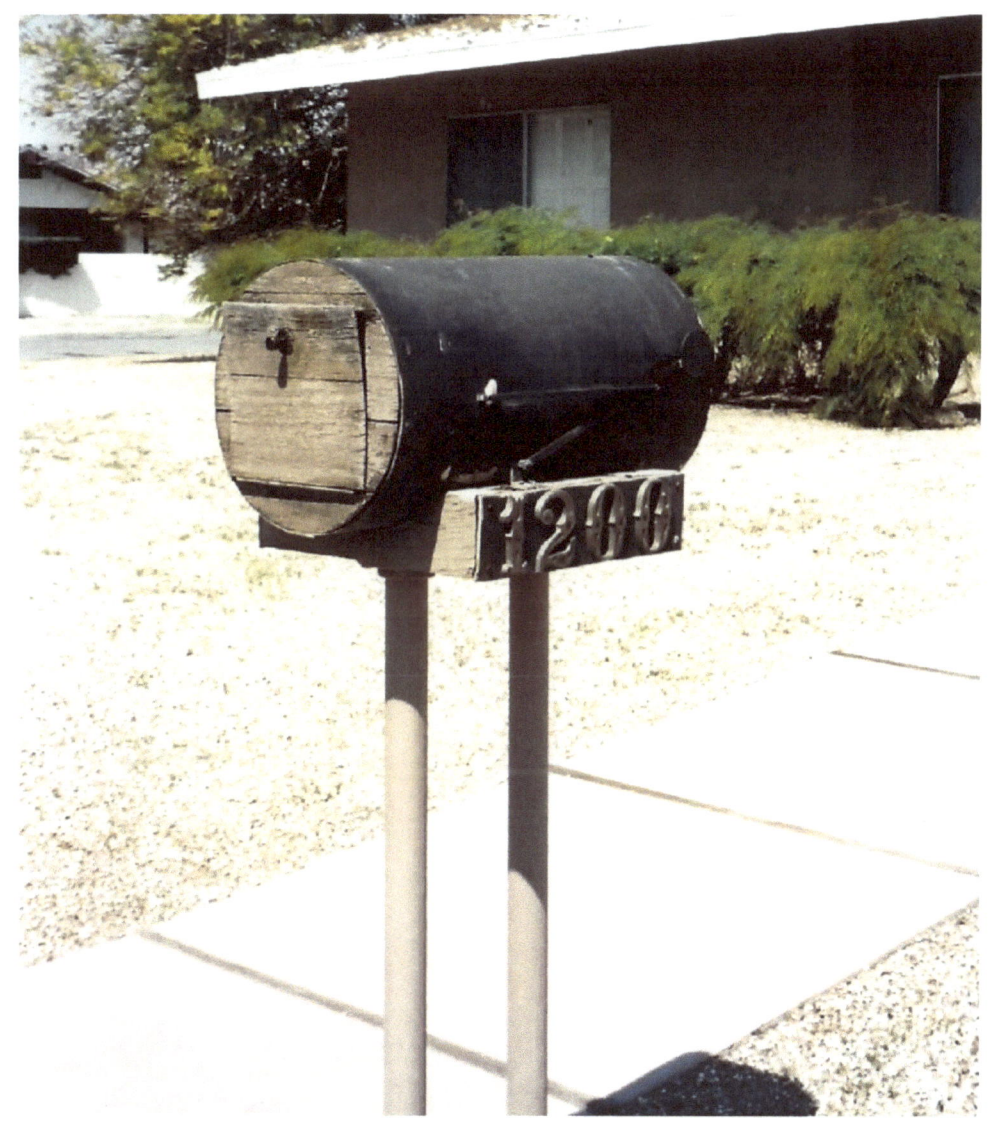

(15)

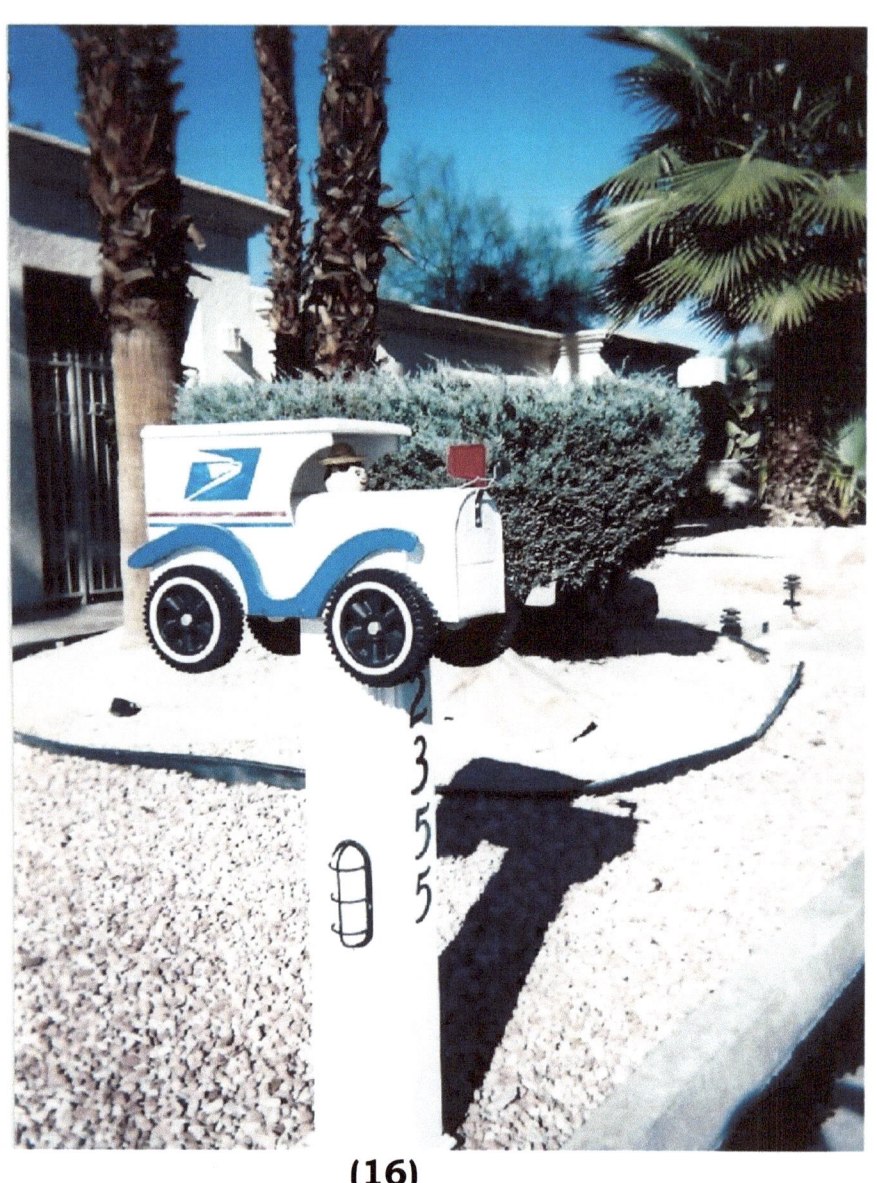

(16)

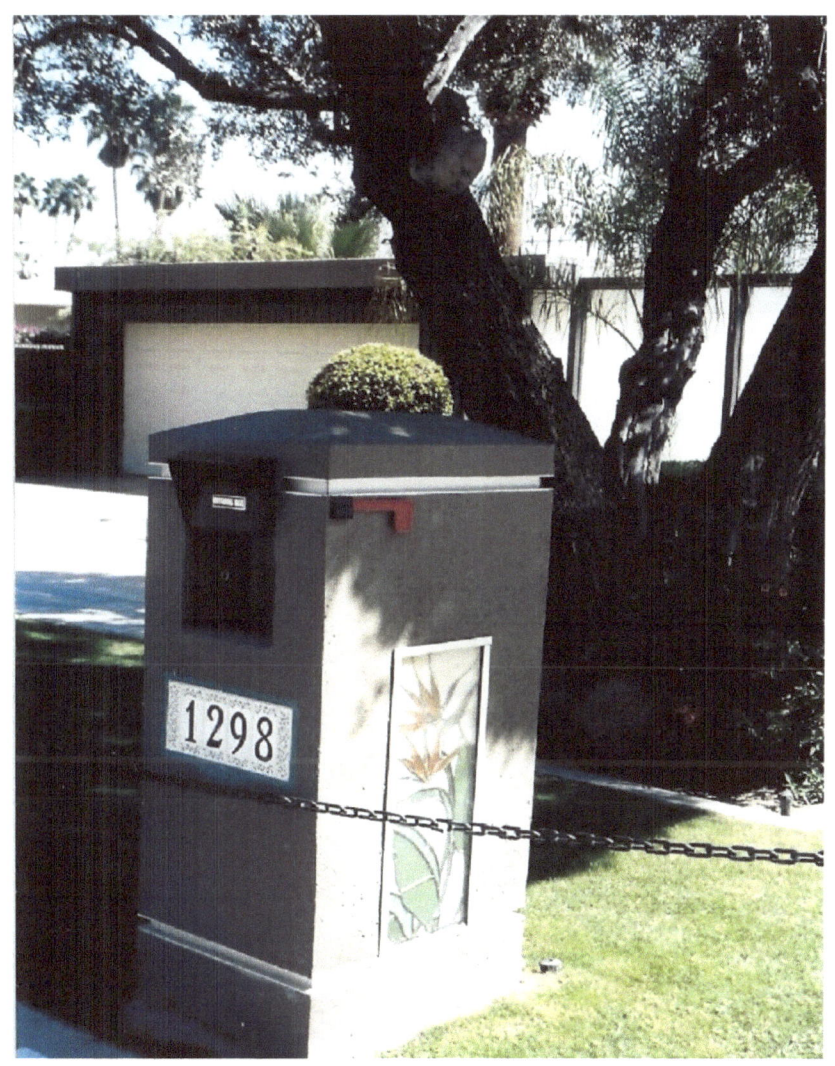

(17)

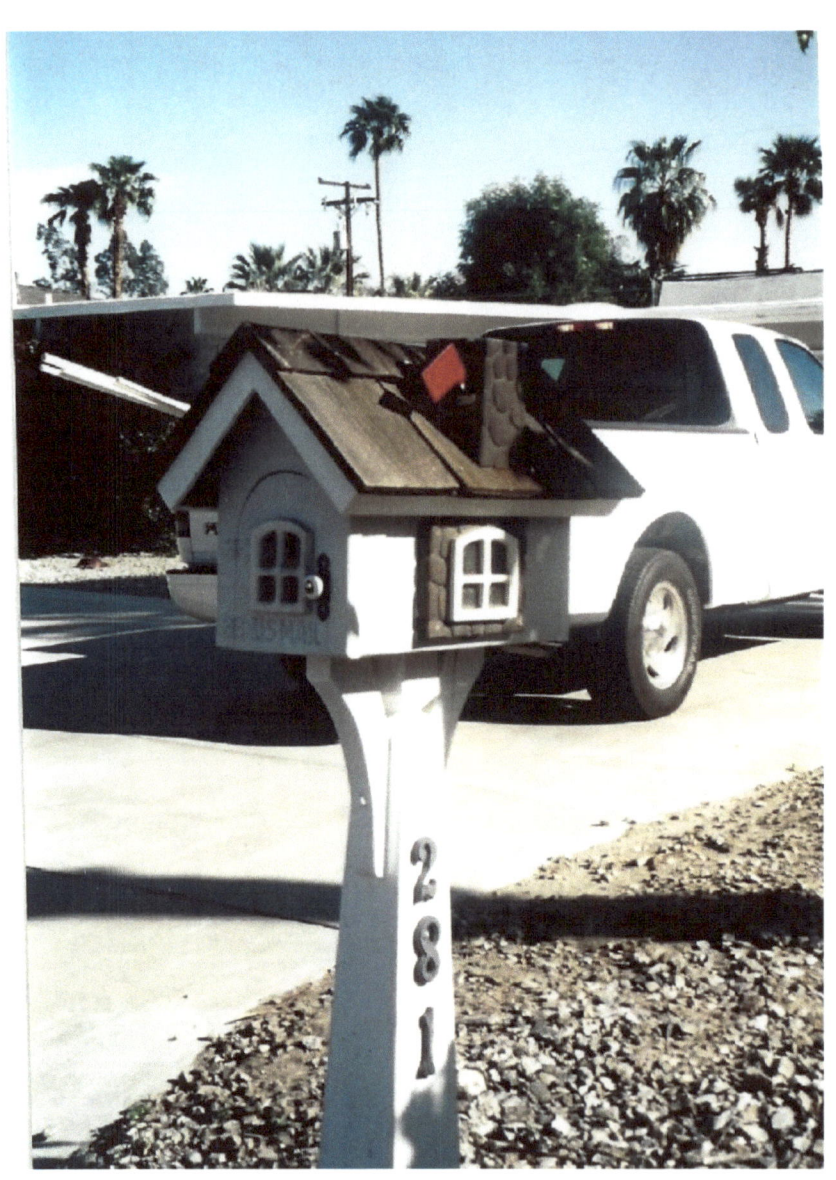

(18)

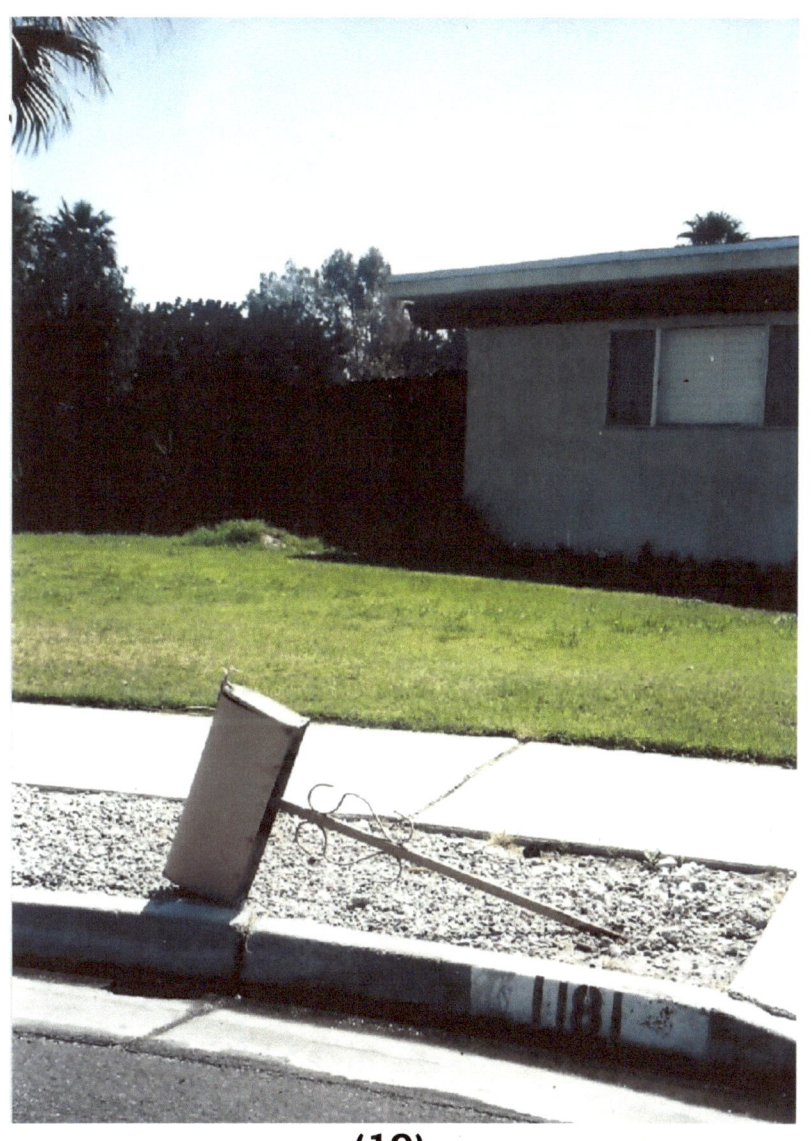

(19)

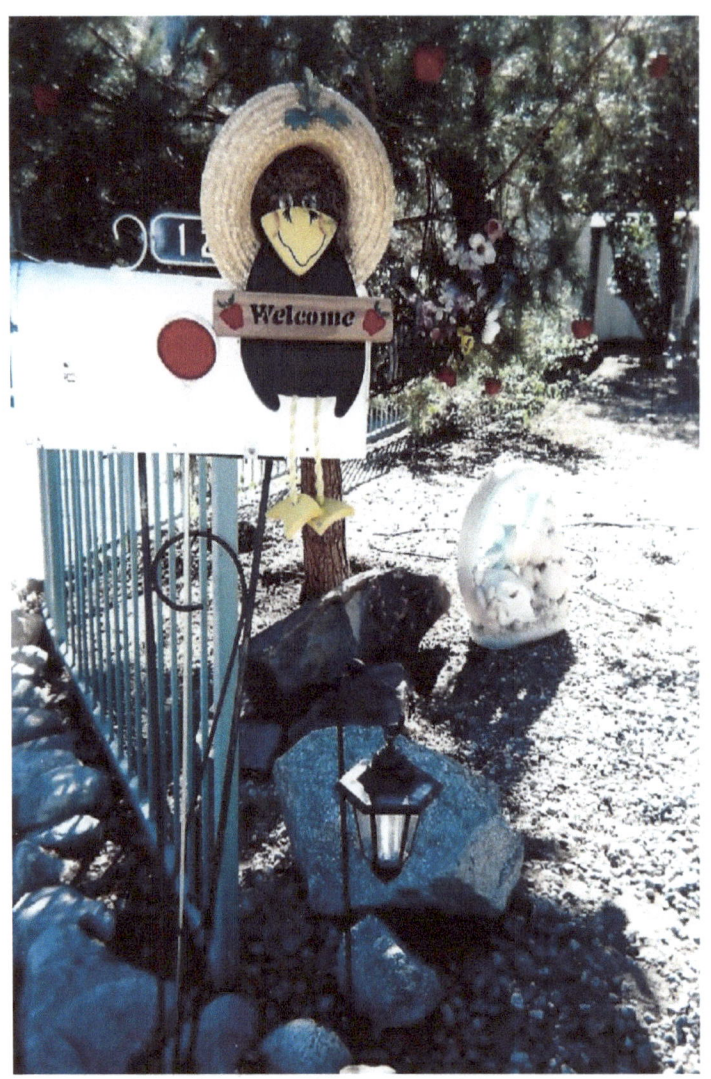

Thank you Mrs. Hubbard
(20)

The End
I Have
Two Hundred and forty five
Photo of Mail Box's